LAUGH
-OUT-
LOUD
JOKES FOR KIDS
DAD
JOKES

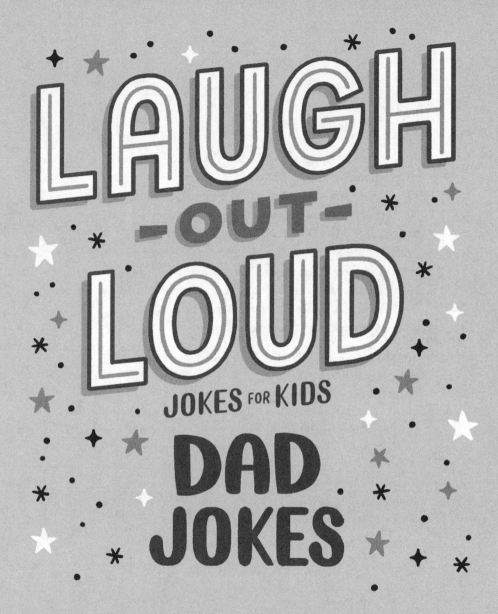

LAUGH -OUT- LOUD

JOKES FOR KIDS

DAD JOKES

ROB ELLIOTT

HARPER

An Imprint of HarperCollinsPublishers

Laugh-Out-Loud: Dad Jokes

Text copyright © 2024 by Robert Elliott Teigen

Illustrations by Catherine Lee

All rights reserved. Printed in the United States of America.
No part of this book may be used or reproduced in
any manner whatsoever without written permission
except in the case of brief quotations embodied in
critical articles and reviews. For information address
HarperCollins Children's Books, a division of HarperCollins
Publishers, 195 Broadway, New York, NY 10007.
www.harpercollinschildrens.com

Library of Congress Control Number: 2023943339
ISBN 978-0-06-328770-9 (paper-over-board)
ISBN 978-0-06-328772-3 (pbk.)

Typography by Catherine Lee
24 25 26 27 28 LBC 5 4 3 2 1

First Edition

LAUGH
-OUT-
LOUD

JOKES FOR KIDS

DAD JOKES

Q: What do hunters drink in the woods?

A: Camo-mile tea!

Q: What did the bee say to its owner?

A: You're a keeper!

Q: What did the cupcake say to the frosting?

A: I'd be muffin without you.

Q: How do kittens bake their cookies?

A: From scratch!

Q: Why did the farmer become a DJ?

A: Because he had some sick beets!

Dad: Life sure has been hard since I gave up soft drinks!

Kid: Why?

Dad: It's soda-pressing.

Q: Why do melons like to have big weddings?

A: Because they cantaloupe!

Dad: Do you know where they made the first french fries?

Kid: France?

Dad: Nope, they cooked them in grease! (Greece)

Q: How do you find out the weather on top of a mountain?

A: You climate!

Q: How often do chemists tell dad jokes?

A: Periodically!

Q: Why did the pepper put on a coat?

A: It was a little chili.

Q: What do you get when you pick a hog's nose?

A: Hamboogers!

Q: Did you hear about the comedian who never left his house?

A: He only told inside jokes.

Q: Why can't you trust a maple tree?

A: Because it's shady!

Q: What do you call a T-rex that always complains?

A: A whine-osaur!

Q: Why did the girl throw away her hula hoop?

A: She thought it was a waist of time.

Q: What happened when the Atlantic Ocean challenged the Pacific Ocean to a race?

A: They tide.

Q: What do you get when you cross a surfboard and a library?

A: A title wave!

Q: What did the almond say to the peanut in a race?

A: I'm going to cashew!

Q: Why did the barista need a vacation from her job?

A: It was a grind!

Q: What's a teacher's favorite drink?

A: Hot chalk-olate!

Q: Did you hear about the cow that saved the world?

A: It was legend-dairy!

Q: What happened when nineteen and twenty got in a fight?

A: Twenty-one!

Q: Did you hear about the criminal who stole a bar of soap?

A: He needed to clean up his act!

Q: Why couldn't the hot peppers practice archery?

A: Because they didn't habanero.

Q: **What do you get when you cross a sheep, a car, and a swimsuit?**

A: A Lamb-bikini!

Q: **What do you call a really bad dad joke?**

A: Pop corn!

Q: **How do ducks play baseball?**

A: They just wing it!

Q: Why shouldn't you pick on your dentist?

A: You might hurt her fillings!

Q: What do dads like to read when they're tired?

A: The snooze-paper.

Q: What happened when the wasp died?

A: It turned into a zom-bee.

Q: How do sheep go to the movies?

A: They take a Ewe-ber!

Q: Why did the book go to the hospital?

A: It had to have its appendix removed.

Q: Why do books feel bullied?

A: People are always judging them by their covers!

Q: Why can't you trust a rubber band?

A: They're always stretching the truth!

Daughter: Dad, do you mind if I call you later?

Dad: I'd rather you call me "Dad"!

Q: What happened when the customer complained about the baker's bread?

A: It got a rise out of him!

Q: Why did the sharks get engaged?

A: They wanted to make it o-fish-ial!

Q: Why did the cowboy move his cows to New York City?

A: He was de-ranged!

Q: What happens when you run out of beans?

A: You're desti-toot!

Q: What happened when the drummer quit the band?

A: There were re-percussions!

Q: What do soldiers wear to the beach?

A: Tank tops.

Q: Why are cowboys so encouraging?

A: They like to spur people on!

Knock, knock.

Who's there?

Canoe.

Canoe who?

Canoe tell me another funny dad joke?

Q: **When is a cow like a cup of coffee?**

A: When it's calf-einated!

Q: **What happened when the cowboy sold all his cattle?**

A: He made a lot of moo-la!

Q: **Why did the clock go on vacation?**

A: It was really wound up!

Dad: You should never brush your teeth with your left hand.

Kid: Why?

Dad: Because a toothbrush works much better!

Q: Why did the fries stay and chat after dinner?

A: They wanted to ketchup!

Q: Where do baby ghosts go in the daytime?

A: Day scare!

Q: Why is it a bad idea to tell booger jokes?

A: Because they're snot funny!

Q: Why did the deer go to the orthodontist?

A: It had buck teeth!

Q: What did Tennessee?

A: The same thing as Arkan-saw!

Q: What do you get when you cross a dinosaur and a poet?

A: Brontë-saurus!

Q: Why did the woman fall in love with the janitor?

A: He swept her off her feet!

Q: What do you call a pumpkin that goes to the gym?

A: A jacked-o'-lantern!

Q: What do you call a snowman with a six-pack?

A: The abdominal snowman.

Q: What do you call a caterpillar that hates Christmas?

A: A bah humbug!

Q: Why did the meteorologist go to the doctor?

A: She was feeling under the weather.

Kid: Dad, will you please put my shoes on?

Dad: I'll try, but I don't think they'll fit me!

Q: What was Santa's favorite subject in school?

A: Geome-tree!

Q: Why can't you get cows to do what you say?

A: It's in one ear and out the udder!

Q: Where do farmers practice their jokes?

A: The funny farm!

Q: Why did the jack-o-lantern go to the gym?

A: It was feeling like a plumpkin.

Q: How do snowmen like their root beer?

A: Frosty!

Q: What do a dog and a watch have in common?

A: They both have ticks!

Q: What is a lazy cook's favorite recipe?

A: Meat loaf!

Kid: What do race-car drivers eat before a big race?

Dad: Nothing—they fast!

Q: What is a gymnast's favorite season?

A: Spring!

Q: What is a cat's favorite dessert?

A: Chocolate mouse!

Q: What do you call it when a snowman throws a tantrum?

A: A meltdown!

Q: Where do boats go when they don't feel well?

A: The dock-tor.

Q: Why didn't the sun want to go to college?

A: It already had a million degrees!

Q: What's a plumber's favorite vegetable?

A: Leeks!

Q: What did the rabbit say to the carrot?

A: It's been nice gnawing you!

Q: What did the garlic do before it took a shower?

A: It took its cloves off!

Q: Why can't you trust a farmer?

A: Because he's always plotting something!

Q: Why was the plant embarrassed?

A: It soiled itself!

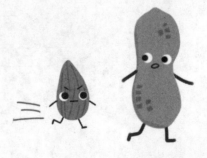

Q: What do you call a number that travels the world?

A: A roaming numeral.

Q: Why was the sailor so average?

A: He was always at "C."

Q: Why did Dracula go to the doctor?

A: He couldn't stop the coffin!

Q: What is a mummy's favorite food?

A: Wraps!

Q: What happened when the Stormtroopers made fun of Darth Vader?

A: It was a dark roast!

Q: What do whales eat for dinner?

A: Fish and ships!

Q: Why can't you win a game of tag with lightning?

A: As soon as you get close, it bolts!

Q: How does a book stay warm?

A: It puts on its jacket!

**Q: What happened when the
alligator swallowed the toad?**

A: It croaked!

**Q: What did the lamp say to the light
bulb?**

A: Watts up?

Q: Why are elves such good listeners?

A: They're all ears!

Dad: "Hello, I think my wife is going to have a baby."

Doctor: "Is this her first child?"

Dad: "No, this is her husband!"

Q: **Why does it cost so much to fly a hot-air balloon?**

A: Inflation!

Q: **Why is a banker like a skunk?**

A: One make cents, and the other makes scents!

Q: Why didn't the turkey have dessert after dinner?

A: Because it was stuffed!

Kid: How much did it cost to fix the roof?

Dad: Nothing—it was on the house!

Q: Where do lumberjacks go when they're tired?

A: For-rest!

Q: Why did the carpenter quit his job?

A: He was board!

Q: What do you get when you cross a cow and a toad?

A: A bullfrog!

Q: How do you know when a cake is sad?

A: When it's in tiers!

Q: Why can't you tell dad jokes in chemistry class?

A: They'll get a bad reaction!

Q: **Why do puppies put you in a good mood?**

A: Because they're so paws-itive!

Q: **Why did the astronauts break up?**

A: They needed space!

Q: **What happened when the tigers got into a fight?**

A: It was cat-astrophic!

Q: What happened when the frog ate all its Halloween candy?

A: It was hopped up on sugar!

Q: Why did the snowman take a nap?

A: It needed to chill out.

Q: Why couldn't the race-car driver pick out new tires?

A: Because he was indy-cisive!

Q: What does a dolphin do when it catches a cold?

A: It takes vitamin sea!

Q: What did the tree say when winter was over?

A: "What a re-leaf!"

Q: How do squirrels stream their favorite shows?

A: On Nutflix.

Dad: Did your mom like the new refrigerator?

Kid: Yes, her face lit up when she opened it!

Q: Why was the pebble so shy?

A: It wasn't a little boulder.

Q: What is the nicest vegetable of all?

A: A sweet potato!

Q: Did you hear about the hot dog that went skydiving?

A: It mustard up the courage to do it!

Q: Why didn't the kids go to the pumpkin patch?

A: They couldn't carve out the time.

Q: Why did the girl get a job at the farm?

A: She needed a stable income.

Q: Why did the scissors get fired?

A: They didn't make the cut.

Q: How do you be sure to make your pants last?

A: Put your shirt and socks on first.

Q: Why can't you trust a train conductor?

A: He has loco-motives!

Q: Why did the belt go to jail?

A: It held up a pair of pants.

Q: What do you get when you cross a vampire and a convertible?

A: A blood drive!

Q: What do you call a fish with two knees?

A: A two-knee fish!

Dad: Where does a composer keep his music?

Kid: In his Bach-pack!

Q: What do you get when you cross dynamite and a block of French cheese?

A: A lot of d'brie everywhere!

Q: What do you call a chicken that comes back to life?

A: A poultry-geist!

Q: Why did the firefly stay up all night?

A: It was a light sleeper!

Q: Why did the toilet paper roll down the hill?

A: It wanted to get to the bottom!

Kid: What do you get when you combine a snowman and a skeleton?

Dad: I don't know, but it's bone-chilling!

Q: What's a zombie's favorite instrument?

A: The organ!

Q: What is black and white and goes "oom"?

A: A cow walking backward!

Q: What is an astronaut's favorite meal of the day?

A: Launch time!

Q: What do you get when you cross a golden retriever and a forest?

A: A fur tree with a lot of bark!

Q: Why did the cat ask for a napkin?

A: It needed to wipe its mouse-stache!

Q: What does Peter Rabbit listen to on the radio?

A: Hip-hop.

Dad: What do dogs have that no other animals have?

Dad: Puppies!

Q: What do you get when winter and autumn are combined?

A: Snowfall.

Q: How did the chicken get to the hospital?

A: In a heli-coop-ter!

Q: What happens if you swallow your watch?

A: You'll get tick to your stomach!

Q: Why do you need an umbrella if you visit England?

A: Because somebody is always reigning there!

Kid: Dad, does money grow on trees?

Dad: No, tomorrow there might be a change in the weather!

Q: What do you call a chicken that lives in the woods?

A: Poul-tree!

Q: Why are barbers never late?

A: They know all the shortcuts!

Poodle: I'd rather have fleas than ticks.

Beagle: To itch their own!

Kid: What's the best way to chop down a tree?

Dad: I'm stumped!

Q: Why do you have to follow the rules at the farm?

A: If you don't, the pigs will squeal on you.

Q: Why did the tree need a doctor?

A: It was a sick-amore!

Q: What do you get when you cross a grasshopper and Santa?

A: Chimney cricket!

Q: Why did the tow truck driver need a vacation?

A: He was a nervous wreck!

Kid: I want to be a train conductor when I grow up!

Dad: Then get good grades and stay on track.

Q: What do you call a potato at a football game?

A: A spec-tater!

Kid: Mom says you have no sense of direction.

Dad: Where did that come from?

Q: Why do fishermen know so many people?

A: They know how to net-work!

Q: What did the vampire wear to the ball?

A: A diamond neck-lace!

Dad: From now on, I'm not going to buy any bandages.

Kid: Why not?

Dad: Because they're a rip-off!

Q: Why do horses get along so well?

A: They're always neigh-borly!

Q: Where did the turtles go when it rained?

A: Into their shell-ter!

Q: Why do bunnies have big ears?

A: So they can hare you better!

Q: Why won't zombies get a job?

A: Because they're deadbeats!

Q: Why don't pigs get invited to parties?

A: Because they're so boar-ing.

Q: Why was the detective spying on the butcher?

A: It was a steakout!

Kid: How can I learn to cook an omelet?

Dad: You just need a good eggsplanation.

Q: Why did the boxer leave the party?

A: He didn't like the punch!

Q: Why couldn't the Dalmatian stop laughing?

A: Because it was tick-lish!

Q: Why do whales always clean up after themselves?

A: They're tide-y!

Q: What happened when the cannibal was late for dinner?

A: He got the cold shoulder!

Q: What is a three-letter word that starts with gas?

A: Car!

Q: Why is the word *dark* spelled with a *K*?

A: Because you can't *C* in the dark!

Q: What do you call two witches who live together?

A: Broommates!

Q: What's a monster's favorite dinner?

A: Spook-etti!

Q: What happened when the gymnasts went on a date?

A: They fell head over heels for each other!

Q: Why did the swimmer want a slingshot for his birthday?

A: He liked to shoot pool!

Q: Where do butchers go to party?

A: The meat ball.

Q: Why was the garbage collector feeling sad?

A: He got dumped!

Kid: Dad, can you call me an Uber?

Dad: You're an Uber!

Q: What is a snowman's favorite game?

A: Freeze tag!

Q: Why do astronauts throw the best parties?

A: Because they're always a blast!

Boy: Dad, have you seen my sunglasses?

Dad: No, have you seen my dad glasses?

Q: Why did the mailman become a comedian?

A: He knew how to deliver a joke!

Q: What kind of tissue can you sleep on?

A: A nap-kin!

Q: What did the princess order at the restaurant?

A: An enchi-lah-dee-dah.

Q: Why did the dentist join the band?

A: He had a tuba toothpaste.

Q: Did you hear about the rabbit who couldn't jump?

A: It needed a hopper-ation!

Q: What is a frog's favorite meal?

A: Prime ribbit.

Q: What happened when the little boy's ice cream melted?

A: He lost his cool!

Q: **Which animals get the most respect?**

A: Giraffes, because everybody is always looking up to them!

Q: **Where is the spookiest place to go fishing?**

A: Lake Erie!

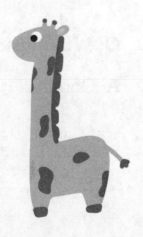

Q: Why did the elephant have a bad time on vacation?

A: The airline lost its trunk!

Q: How do you keep people from stealing your bagels?

A: With lox!

Q: What kind of keys are edible?

A: Cookies!

Dad: Do you think I could get a wig for free?

Kid: No, you have toupee for it.

Dad: Why did you eat all the pickles?

Kid: Because they're dill-icious!

Q: What do you call a chair made of pine?

A: Fir-niture!

Q: Why don't ducks play baseball?

A: They hit too many fowl balls.

Q: Where do snails keep their clothes when they travel?

A: In their sluggage!

Q: What do baseball players eat on their birthday?

A: Bunt cake!

Q: Why couldn't the detective find the missing snowman?

A: It was a cold case!

Q: Why can't you trust a sloth?

A: They're always lying around.

Dad: Do you want to hear my joke about the tire?

Kid: No!

Dad: Are you sure? It's wheel-y funny!

Q: Why did the panda turn up the music?

A: Because it could bearly hear it.

Q: How do you get a boulder to sleep?

A: Sing "Rock-a-Bye Baby."

Q: What do you get when you cross a squirrel and a turtle?

A: A nutshell!

Dad: Did you hear about the rancher that planted a whole field of beans?

Kid: No, what happened?

Dad: He was a rootin'-tootin' cowboy!

Q: What is a lumberjack's favorite kind of comedy?

A: Slapstick!

Q: Why are skeletons always so calm?

A: Nothing gets under their skin.

Q: How do you get in touch with Saturn?

A: You give it a ring!

Q: What is a zombie's favorite candy bar?

A: Butterfingers!

Q: What do you get when you combine a bird and a bee?

A: A buzz-ard!

Q: How did the Italian chef fix his broken noodle?

A: With tomato paste!

Q: What do dads and mushrooms have in common?

A: They're both fungi!

Q: What is a zombie's favorite food?

A: Raw-man noodles!

Q: What kind of exercises should lazy people do?

A: Diddly-squats!

Q: How did the shellfish know it had a fever?

A: It was clammy!

Q: When can't you trust a candle?

A: When it's wick-ed.

Kid: Dad, how do I look?

Dad: With your eyes!

Q: Where does a loaf of bread rise?

A: In the yeast!

Q: How can a farmer get his wife's attention?

A: A tractor!

Q: Where do cats like to go on vacation?

A: To the meow-ntains.

Q: Did you hear about the race between the lettuce and tomato?

A: The lettuce was a "head," and the tomato was trying to "ketchup"!

Q: What did the zombie say to his girlfriend?

A: You're drop-dead gorgeous!

Q: What do monsters like to drink in the fall?

A: Apple spider!

Q: What do Santa and websites have in common?

A: They both have cookies!

Q: Why did the girl wear mittens to the dance?

A: It was a snow ball.

Q: Why can't you believe a chicken?

A: It always eggs-aggerates.

Q: Where does a pilot keep her uniform?

A: On a hangar.

Q: How did the computer keep from getting a virus?

A: It got a screen shot.

93

Q: What kind of smell keeps going up and up?

A: Ascent!

Dad: What is the biggest state in America?

Kid: Alaska teacher and let you know.

Q: What is the most inexpensive car?

A: Af-ford!

Q: Why did the archer drop out of school?

A: Because he was aimless.

Q: What did the hamburger say to the steak?

A: I've got a beef with you!

Q: Why are baby goats so funny?

A: They're always kid-ding around!

Q: Why wouldn't the actor take off his costume after work?

A: It was a stage he was going through.

Q: Where did the frogs find true love?

A: Under the mistle-toad.

Q: **Why did Santa buy so many reindeer?**

A: Because they didn't cost much doe!

Q: **What is a whale's favorite treat?**

A: Blubber gum!

Q: **Why don't squirrels like chipmunks?**

A: Because they drive them nuts!

Q: What did the witch do when she was tired?

A: She sat for a spell.

Q: How did the skunk get a trophy?

A: It won the smelling bee!

Q: Why did the fish go on vacation?

A: He was tired of being in school all the time.

Q: Why did the apple join the gym?

A: To work on its core!

Q: Why did the tiger get fired?

A: It was always lion around on the
job!

Kid: Dad, where are you from?

Dad: My parents!

Q: What happened when the witch fell off the broom and broke her arm?

A: She wore a cast for a spell!

Q: Which planet has the best music?

A: Nep-tune!

Q: Why did the janitor mop the gym?

A: The basketball players were dribbling.

Q: Why was the chicken always telling jokes?

A: It was a comedi-hen!

Q: What are the strongest creatures in the ocean?

A: Mussels!

Q: What do polar bears wear to bed?

A: Their paw-jamas!

Q: How do rabbits stay cool in the summer?

A: They turn on the hare conditioning!

Q: Why did the rancher buy so many cows?

A: Because they were afforda-bull.

Q: What is a lumberjack's favorite month?

A: Sep-timber!

Q: Why are bakers so smart?

A: They're always on the honor roll.

Q: Did you hear about the spoon and blender that got married?

A: They caused quite a stir!

Q: Where do bakers go to school?

A: In Colora-dough!

Q: Which muscle is the first to go?

A: Your bye-cep!

Q: Why did the boy take his bucket to the doctor?

A: It looked a little pail!

Q: What did Jack Frost say after he got new glasses?

A: "I-cy!"

Q: Why do mummies feel nervous at Christmas?

A: All the unwrapping!

Q: Why did the pony get in trouble?

A: It kept horsing around!

Q: What do you call spiders after they get married?

A: Newly-webs!

Q: What did the tailor do when she saw the door was open?

A: She clothed it!

Q: What was written on the robot's gravestone?

A: Rust in Peace

Q: What is the best time of year to practice addition?

A: Sum-mer!

Dad: You know why I love cheese jokes?

Kid: Why?

Dad: Because they're grate!

Q: What kind of cheese do basketball players put on their sandwiches?

A: Swish cheese!

Kid: How do I know if I put the right amount of frosting on your cake?

Dad: You find the sweet spot.

Kid: Prices of balloons are really going up!

Dad: Must be inflation!

Q: Did you hear about the fig and the raisin?

A: They went on a date!

Q: Why did the mechanic go out of business?

A: He got wheely tired of it!

Q: What did the salad say before dinner?

A: Lettuce pray!

Q: How do you know if a burrito is upset?

A: You don't—they won't taco 'bout their fillings.

Q: What do you get when you cross a ghost and a tortilla?

A: A boo-rrito!

Kid: The restaurant says they're short-staffed.

Dad: That's not fair to tall people!

Q: What did the salt say to the pepper?

A: "See you next season!"

Q: What did one pickle say to the other pickle when it fell on the ground?

A: Dill with it!

Q: Why did the elephant quit the circus?

A: It was tired of working for peanuts!

Dad: I used to have a fear of jumping over fences.

Kid: You did?

Dad: Yep, but I got over it!

Q: What do you call a fake alligator?

A: A crock-odile!

Q: Why did the grandfather clock go on vacation?

A: So it could unwind!

Kid: I got all dirty making mud pies.

Dad: You're grounded!

Q: Why did the cat go to the doctor?

A: He wasn't feline well!

Dad: Why doesn't anyone laugh at skeleton jokes?

Kid: They're not humerus!

Dad: Did you hear about the Italian chef who ate too many noodles?

Kid: He pasta-way!

Q: Where do trees invest their money?

A: In a hedge fund!

Q: How do beavers read their email?

A: They log in!

Q: Why did the tree go to the hairstylist?

A: It wanted to color its roots!

Q: Why did the horse always buck off the cowboy?

A: He got a kick out of it!

Q: Why is it hard to rest at a cattle ranch?

A: Because all the bulls have horns!

Dad: Did I tell you the joke about the cattle ranch?

Kid: Yes, I already herd it.

Q: What's a ghost's favorite story?

A: Winnie the Boo!

Q: Why did the paper go to the gym?

A: It wanted to get ripped!

Q: How do you know when a whale is sad?

A: When it's blubbering!

Q: Why don't lizards know how much they weigh?

A: Because they're always losing their scales!

Q: Where is the worst place to buy a dog?

A: At the flea market!

Q: What is Frosty's favorite Christmas carol?

A: "The First Snow-el"!

Q: What kind of cars do the nicest people drive?

A: Care-avans!

Dad: Do you want to be a fisherman when you grow up?

Kid: Yes, if I get the oppor-tuna-ty!

Q: What's a landscaper's favorite kind of music?

A: Bluegrass!

Q: How did the pig get to the hospital?

A: In the hambulance!

Dad: What did the baby zebra say to the piano?

Kid: "Play some music"?

Dad: No, "Dad, is that you?"

Dad: Does money grow on trees?

Kids: Nope!

Dad: Then why do banks have branches?

Dad: Did you know people eat more bananas than monkeys?

Kid: That's not possible!

Dad: When was the last time you saw a person eat a monkey?

Q: **What did the mommy deer say to her baby?**

A: I'm fawn-ed of you!

Q: **Why aren't giraffes very funny?**

A: Their jokes are always over your head!

Dad: How do I stop telling Thanksgiving jokes?

Kid: You just quit cold turkey.

Dad: What color is the wind?

Kid: It's blew!

Q: What do yellow jackets do when they have to go potty?

A: They make a beeline for the bathroom!

Q: Why was the baker stressed about money?

A: She was the only breadwinner in the family!

Q: What do you call grumpy bread?

A: Sourdough!

Q: Why wouldn't the turtle and the snail talk to each other?

A: Neither of them would come out of their shell.

Dad: I think you should be quiet.

Kid: Why?

Dad: Never mind, it's a mute point.

Q: Did you hear about the two baristas who fell in love?

A: It was a brew-tiful love story.

Dad: Don't tell me any jokes about gravity.

Kid: Why not?

Dad: Because I fall for them every single time!

Q: Why do gardeners make great detectives?

A: Because they always get to the root of the problem!

Q: What do pilots like to order at restaurants?

A: Hot wings!

Q: What kind of car does a chicken drive?

A: A Yolkswagen!

Q: Where do female astronauts like to go?

A: Into the gal-axy!

Q: What do elephants like to eat for dinner?

A: Smashed potatoes!

Q: What's big, green, and sits crying in the corner?

A: The Incredible Sulk!

Q: What happened to the witch when she got in trouble at school?

A: She was ex-spelled!

Q: How do you get your builder's license?

A: You have to nail the exam.

Q: What do you get when you combine a centipede and a parrot?

A: A walkie-talkie!

Kid: I forgot where I put my boomerang.

Dad: I'm sure it will come back to you.

Q: How did the painter stay warm?

A: He put on another coat.

Kid: Who makes the very best pants in the world?

Dad: I don't know, but they must be a jean-ius.

Q: What do you call an owl who's a magician?

A: Hoooo-dini.

Q: How do ghosts like their eggs?

A: Terri-fried!

Q: What do you get if you put dynamite in a chicken coop?

A: A huge eggs-plosion!

Q: What did the baby computer call his father?

A: Data!

Q: Did you hear about the snowman who got hit with a snowball?

A: He was knocked out cold!

Q: What kind of lid is always best to keep on?

A: An eyelid!

Q: Why did the cow take its babies to the gym?

A: It wanted to work its calves!

Mom: I just got my genetic test results and I'm 100 percent Scandinavian!

Dad: There is Norway that can be right!

Kid: The dog got sprayed by a skunk!

Dad: That stinks.

Q: Why do plumbers like to sing?

A: Because they have nice pipes!

**Kid: What should I eat if I want to
run really fast?**

Dad: Eat your legumes!

Q: What did the turtle sing at the talent show?

A: "Shell Be Comin' Round the Mountain."

Q: Why did the painter get arrested?

A: He was a con artist!

Q: How does Dracula fight off his enemies?

A: Hand-to-hand com-bat!

Q: Why do boxers like dad jokes so much?

A: They love a good punch line!

Q: Why do burgers taste better in space?

A: Because they're meat-eor!

Q: **Why wouldn't the cat eat its dinner?**

A: There was something fishy about it.

Q: **Why did the monster need a tissue?**

A: He was the boogeyman!

Q: How many golfers does it take to change a light bulb?

A: Fore!

Q: What language does a goose speak?

A: Portu-geese.

Q: What do penguins like on their tacos?

A: Chilly sauce!

Q: Why did the baker go to the square dance?

A: She wanted to dough-si-dough!

Q: When can you put a canoe on your head?

A: When it's cap-sized!

Q: Where does a clown go to dance?

A: To the goof ball!

Q: Why was Santa late on Christmas Eve?

A: He got the flue!

Q: Why couldn't Bach pay for his dinner?

A: Because he was Baroque!

Q: Why did the cantaloupe jump into the lake?

A: It wanted to be a watermelon!

Q: How did Jack feel after chopping down the beanstalk?

A: Vine and dandy.

Dad: Did you have fun going fishing?

Kid: Yes, I'm hooked!

Q: How do horses drink their milk?

A: Through a straw!

Q: Why did the clock get detention?

A: Because it tocked too much in class.

Q: Why was the cobra embarrassed?

A: It realized it was snake-ed!

Q: Why was the sneaker so sad?

A: It lost its sole mate!

Q: How fast does the Grinch's sleigh go?

A: "Max" speed!

Q: Why did the boy eat the dictionary?

A: He wanted to be a smart-mouth!

Q: Why did the beaver wake up so happy?

A: Because it slept like a log!

Q: Why did the tree have so many friends?

A: It was poplar!

Q: Why are zombies always so punctual?

A: They never miss a dead-line.

Q: Why aren't pretzels very funny?

A: They have a twisted sense of humor.

Q: What did the fox eat for a snack?

A: Geese and crackers.

Q: What happened when the ship ran into an iceberg?

A: The sailors made a salad!

Q: Why did the lemon go to the hospital?

A: It needed some lemon-aid!

Q: Why did the police officer go to the coffee shop?

A: He wanted a mug shot!

Q: What are a dad's four best words of wisdom?

A: "Go ask your mom!"

Q: What did the polar bears do after they got married?

A: They had chill-dren!

Q: Why did the man fall into the hole?

A: He couldn't see that well.

Kid: Want to hear my joke about the sausage?

Dad: No, those are the wurst!

Dad: Why wouldn't any of the kids take the school bus to school.

Kid: Because they had another ride?

Dad: No, it wouldn't fit through the door!

Doctor: I have to remove one of your organs.

Patient: You're kidney-ing me!

Q: How did the pet store sell all their turtles?

A: They had a catchy slow-gan!

Kid: Did I tell you I got lost in the woods again?

Dad: That's path-etic.

Kid: Could you please put out my candle?

Dad: I'd be de-lighted!

Q: Why did the owl drop out of school?

A: It didn't give a hoot.

Kid: My dog can catch a Frisbee from three hundred yards away.

Dad: That sounds far-fetched.

Q: Why did the kid quit the band?

A: He thought it was humdrum.

Q: Did you hear about the skunk who smelled like a rose?

A: That's non-scents!

Kid: I ate my whole grilled-cheese sandwich.

Dad: Gouda for you!

Kid: Why did you give away all our furniture?

Dad: It was for chair-ity!

Kid: Did you hear about the bear in the horror movie?

Dad: Yes, it was grizzly!

Q: Did you hear about the housekeeper who fell in love with the janitor?

A: It was dust-iny!

Q: What kind of instrument comes in a bag?

A: A sacks-ophone!

Q: What kind of dog is always crying?

A: The chi-waa-waa.

Dad: I'm sorry, but you can't go to the carnival.

Kid: That's not fair!

Q: Why was the farmer arrested?

A: He was disturbing the peas.

Kid: Dad, can I make my lemonade stand?

Dad: No, lemonade doesn't have any legs.

Q: What do you get when you cross a pig and a yo-yo?

A: A hamstring!

Q: What did the electrician say to the plumber?

A: Let's switch!

Kid: Dad, will you buy me some bread?

Dad: Sorry, I ran out of dough.

Dad: What's the difference between boogers and broccoli?

Kid: I don't know.

Dad: Kids won't eat their broccoli!

Q: Did you hear about the barfing contest?

A: It was a throw-up throwdown.

Kid: Did you see all the fog this morning?

Dad: No, I mist it.

Q: Why would you drink soda at the gym?

A: To help you with your burpees!

Q: Why was the shark showing off?

A: It was fishing for compliments.

Q: How do grizzlies catch fish for dinner?

A: With their bear hands!

Q: Why were the scissors mad at the knife?

A: They couldn't get a word in edgewise.

Q: **What do sea monsters eat for lunch?**

A: Ships and salsa!

Q: **What happened when the berries spilled in the road?**

A: It caused a traffic jam!

Q: Why did the deer need a coat?

A: It was buck naked!

Q: What kind of bird never gives up?

A: A peli-can!

Q: What is a boxer's favorite meal of the day?

A: Break-fist!

Q: Why did the weatherman eat steak every night?

A: He was a meat-eorologist.

Kid: Dad, I broke my sister's glasses.

Dad: You'd better apolog-eyes!

Q: Why do leopards lose at hide-and-seek?

A: They're too easy to spot.

Kid: Did you like your book about Rapunzel?

Dad: It was a letdown.

Q: What do you get if you're sleepy in art class?

A: Cray-yawns!

Q: How did Little Miss Muffet pay for her lunch?

A: She used her credit curds.

Q: What do you call it when a kitten lunges at a dog?

A: A cat-a-pult!

Q: What do Mickey and Minnie like to do in the winter?

A: Go mice-skating!

Q: What did the lightning say when it was running late?

A: "I'd better bolt!"

Q: Why did Jack Frost get straight A's in school?

A: It was a breeze!

Q: What kind of shoes do cows wear?

A: Meat loafers!

Knock, Knock.

Who's there?

Watson.

Watson who?

Watson on your mind today?

Q: **What does a cowgirl keep in her purse?**

A: ChapStick!

Q: **Why did the mummy show up late for the party?**

A: He got tied up!

Kid: Dad, you make the best corn in the world!

Dad: Aw, shucks.

Q: When is the best time to buy a boat?

A: When they go on sail!

Kid: Dad, let me make you some coffee.

Dad: Thanks a latte!

Q: Why was the goblin sad?

A: He didn't have a ghoul-friend!

Q: What kind of pants does the Hunchback of Notre-Dame wear?

A: Bell-bottoms!

Q: Why did the German shepherd go to jail?

A: Too many unpaid barking tickets!

Q: What did Frosty name his daughter?

A: Snow White!

Q: What do you call a sleepy cow?

A: A bulldozer!

Q: What happened when the frogs got married?

A: They lived hopp-ily ever after!

Q: What's a dog's favorite toy?

A: A pup-pet!

Q: How can you learn more about kittens?

A: Listen to a pawed-cast!

Q: How does the sun say hello?

A: It gives a heat wave!

Q: What happened when the baker and butcher got together?

A: They were bakin' bacon.

Q: Why did the pirate reveal his treasure map?

A: He wanted to get it off his chest.

Dad: Did you hear my joke about the pizza?

Kid: I thought it was cheesy.

Dad: I thought it was grate!

Q: How did Tinkerbell make her breakfast?

A: In Peter's Pan.

Q: Why did the kids play catch with a clock?

A: Because time flies when you're having fun!

Q: Why couldn't the mummy solve the math problem?

A: It couldn't wrap its head around it.

Q: What did one innkeeper say to the other?

A: Your guest is as good as mine.

Q: What did the moon say to the sun?

A: Don't give up your day job.

Q: Why did the queen serve the tea?

A: Because when it reigns it pours.

Kid: What did you think of the new carpet?

Dad: I was floored!

Kid: Do you want to play jump rope?

Dad: Let's skip it.

Q: What kind of rodent lives at the North Pole?

A: A chin-chill-a!

Kid: Do you like my painting of the Mona Lisa?

Dad: It looks art-ificial to me.

Q: Why wouldn't the girl wind up her toy?

A: It made her cranky.

Kid: What will happen if you go barefoot to work?

Dad: I might get the boot!

Q: Why did the granny lose all her yarn?

A: She was a knit-wit.

Q: What does a snake do when it gets a headache?

A: It takes an asp-irin.

Q: Why did the boy stand on his watch?

A: So he could be on time.

Q: What did Santa drink at the parade?

A: A root beer float!

Q: Why did the pilot lose his job?

A: He wouldn't stop com-plane-ing.

Kid: I hung all the candy canes on

the Christmas tree!

Dad: What an achieve-mint!

Teacher: Why won't you sharpen

your pencil?

Kid: I don't see the point.

Guy #1: I'm so sad I didn't meet a girl in Scotland.

Guy #2: A-lass.

Kid: When can we go sailing?

Dad: Schooner or later.

Kid: Can I get a puppy? Can I get a puppy? Can I get a puppy?

Dad: Stop hounding me!

Q: What do you call a tricky chicken?

A: A ruse-ster!

Kid: Nobody cooks from scratch anymore.

Dad: It's a sign of the thymes.

Q: What do you call a squirrel in a monastery?

A: A chip-monk.

Q: Why did the whale go to summer school?

A: It got all seas (C's)!

Q: How many birds can fit in a nest?

A: Toucan!

Q: What do you call a tiny otter?

A: A wee-sel.

Q: Why did the hockey player miss the game?

A: He came down with chicken pucks.

Dad: Would you like some grapes?

Kid: Yes, I like them a bunch.

Dad: How was your grade on your astronomy test?

Kid: It was stellar!

Kid: Why didn't you buy any celery at the store?

Dad: They were out of stalk!

Dad #1: I got a job at the planetarium!

Dad #2: Things are really looking up for you.

Kid: Guess what, we're going to Idaho!

Dad: Oh Boise!

Q: How do you build a big, big boat?

A: You hire an ark-itect.

Q: What kind of bugs are good at math?

A: Account-ants!

Q: Why did the tailor have so many friends?

A: He was very sew-cial!

Kid: Please be sure to remember my bubble gum.

Dad: I got chew!

Kid: Why did the dog eat your phone?

Dad: He had a big app-etite.

Kid: Can we go to the playground today?

Dad: If we can swing it.

Q: Where does a weight lifter go for dinner?

A: To the buff-et.

Q: Why was the police officer taking a nap?

A: Because he was ar-rest-ing.

Knock, knock.

Who's there?

Sherlock.

Sherlock who?

I'll Sherlock the door before I go.